# I ♥ DINOSAURS™

# THE SPIKE-TAILED DINOSAUR

## Stegosaurus

Written and illustrated by
# Michael Berenstain

A GOLDEN BOOK • NEW YORK
Western Publishing Company, Inc., Racine, Wisconsin 53404

Many of the dinosaurs that lived long ago were strange-looking creatures. Some had long necks and tails. Others had huge heads with jaws full of pointed teeth. Many had sharp claws on their feet and odd horns on their heads.

But the strangest-looking dinosaur of all was...

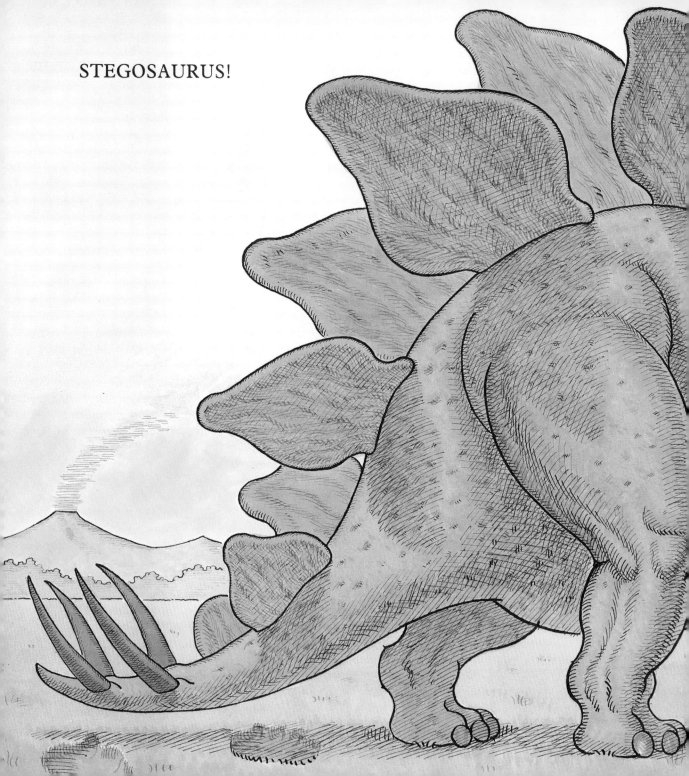

STEGOSAURUS!

Stegosaurus (steg-o-SAW-rus) had a tiny head and a huge body. It could have grown as large as 24 feet long and 12 feet tall. The long spikes on its tail and the large flat plates all along its back set Stegosaurus apart from most other dinosaurs.

Ever since scientists discovered Stegosaurus, they have wondered why it had those odd features.

Stegosaurus probably used its sharp tail spikes to protect itself from large meat-eating dinosaurs like Ceratosaurus (ser-a-toe-SAW-rus). When attacked, Stegosaurus could swing its tail to chase the meat-eater away.

Stegosaurus' back plates may have been used to cool the giant dinosaur when it got too hot. A cool breeze blowing across the plates could have carried heat away from Stegosaurus' body.

Stegosaurus also had a horny beak that it used to pull up the plants it ate. Stegosaurus' teeth were small but sharp, and the dinosaur used them to chop its food into tiny pieces.

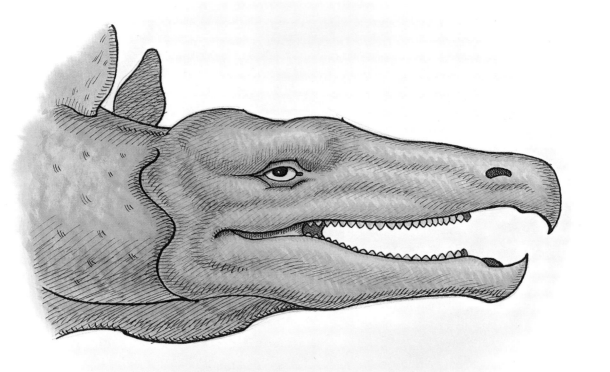

Stegosaurus' giant body needed a lot of food. But its mouth was very small, so it must have had to eat nearly all the time to get enough food.

Inside Stegosaurus' small head was a very small brain. It was no bigger than a golf ball. Compared to other dinosaurs, Stegosaurus may have had one of the smallest brains for its body size.

Tyrannosaurus
(tuh-ran-uh-SAW-rus)

Iguanodon
(i-GWAN-uh-don)

Triceratops
(try-SAIR-uh-tops)

Stegosaurus may have had a tiny brain, but it
had large nerve bundles in its shoulders and
hips. These helped Stegosaurus move the
muscles in its legs and tail quickly and easily.

Stegosaurus was not the only strange-looking dinosaur in the stegosaur family.

Tuojiangosaurus (too-hwang-uh-SAW-rus) was similar to Stegosaurus, but its back plates were long and narrow.

Kentrosaurus (ken-truh-SAW-rus) was smaller than other stegosaurs, but it had many long spikes on its body. It may have used them to defend itself just as a porcupine uses its sharp quills today.

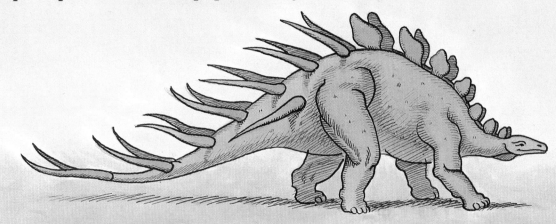

Scelidosaurus (sel-uh-doe-SAW-rus) may have been the ancestor of all the other stegosaurs. It had many small back plates but no spikes.

Scientists first discovered the bones of Stegosaurus more than a hundred years ago in the Western United States.

At first scientists weren't sure just how Stegosaurus' plates were arranged on its back. They had a lot of different ideas. Many scientists now believe that Stegosaurus' plates were in two overlapping rows.

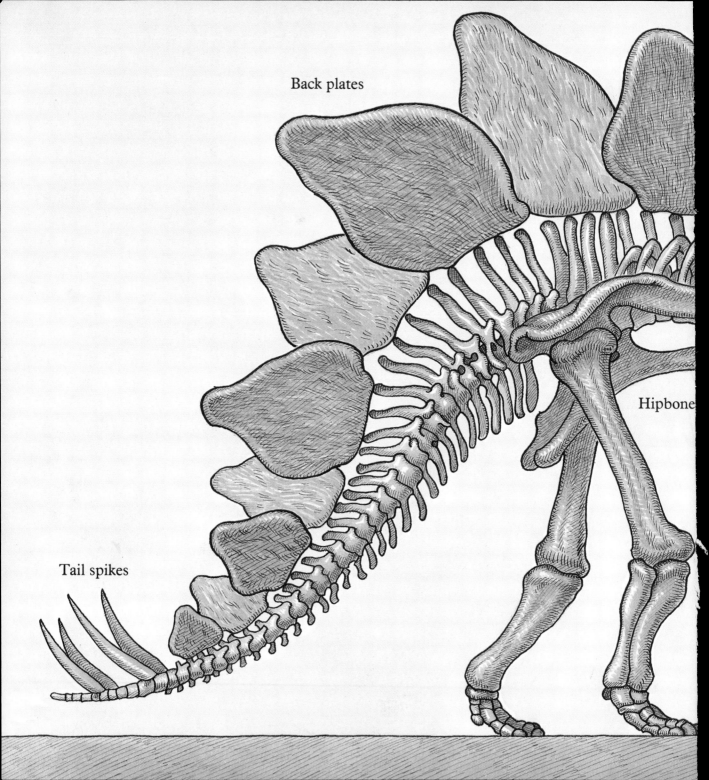

Back plates

Hipbone

Tail spikes

Scientists eventually decided that
Stegosaurus' skeleton looked like this:

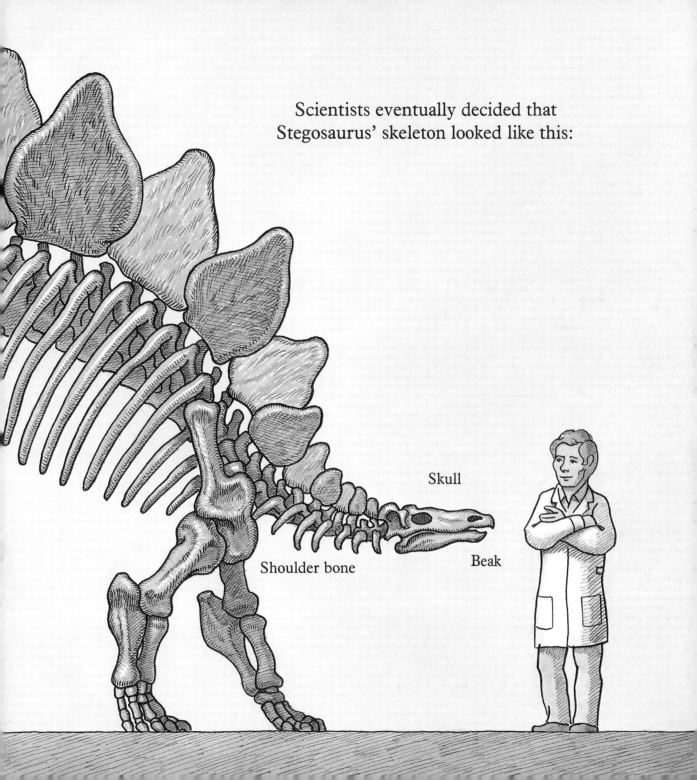

Skull

Shoulder bone

Beak

While Stegosaurus was large, probably slow, and perhaps not too bright, there were other animals in its world that were small, quick, and smart. These were the early mammals. They looked something like mice or opossums with long tails and furry bodies.

These mammals may have helped kill off the dinosaurs by stealing and eating their eggs.

Most of the stegosaurs did not live
till the end of the age of dinosaurs.

They may have been crowded out by the ankylosaurs (ang-KI-lo-sawrs). These armored dinosaurs were much like stegosaurs and could have eaten the food that the stegosaurs needed.

The only stegosaur to survive until the end of the age of dinosaurs was Dravidosaurus (dra-vid-o-SAW-rus). Dravidosaurus lived in what is now the country of India. At that time, India was an island, where there were no ankylosaurs to push the stegosaurs out. Here, the last of the stegosaurs may have lived and died.